SCHOLASTIC

Week-by-Week Homework for Building
Reading Comprehension
and Fluency

30 Reproducible High-Interest Readings for Kids to Read Aloud at Home—With Companion Activities

GRADE 1

BY MARY ROSE

New York • Toronto • London • Auckland • Sydney
Mexico City • New Delhi • Hong Kong • Buenos Aires

DEDICATION

To Dr. Donna Ruth Francis, Ph.D., the best little sister ever

ACKNOWLEDGMENTS

Special thanks to Tom Rose, my ever patient husband

And to Alida Hanna and Nicole Roessle of Lake Sybelia Elementary School;
and Brenda Huckin, of Oxford, England

And to Terry Cooper, Joanna Davis-Swing,
and Merryl Maleska Wilbur of Scholastic Inc.

CREDITS

"The Grasshopper" by David McCord. Reprinted from FAR AND FEW by David McCord.
Copyright © 1952 by David McCord. Reprinted by permission of Little, Brown and Company.

"Monty" by Brenda Huckin is reprinted with permission of the author.

Research cited is based on information in:

Allington, Richard L. *What Really Matters for Struggling Reader.* New York: Addison Wesley Longman, 2001.

Allington, Richard L. and Patricia M. Cunningham.
Schools That Work: Where All Children Read and Write. New York: HarperCollins, 1996.

Cover design by Jason Robinson
Interior design by Solutions by Design, Inc.
Interior illustrations (fiction and poetry) by Maxie Chambliss
Interior illustrations (nonfiction) by Teresa Southwell

ISBN: 0-439-61656-5

Contents

Introduction

I n 1999, facing a fourth-grade classroom of struggling readers, I came up with a homework project aimed at increasing the amount of time my students spent reading aloud. A great deal of research (Allington and Cunningham) has shown that students need far more "read out loud" experiences than the typical classroom can give them. Each week, I assigned my students at the Lake Sybelia Elementary School in Maitland, Florida, a passage to read out loud at home to an adult, along with a set of questions to answer. Each of the questions was directly tied to a state standard or benchmark for language arts. To make it easier for parents to be part of the teaching process, I addressed a letter to them each week explaining the assignment so they could better assist their child.

This concept proved to be so successful that I shared it in workshops with other teachers across the country. Eventually, the book *Week-by-Week Homework for Building Reading Comprehension and Fluency, Grades 3–6* (Scholastic, 2002) evolved. Classroom teachers in those grades found it so helpful that a miniseries has now come about— a similar book aimed at Grades 2–3, along with *this* book, which is specifically targeted to Grade 1 readers. Research (Allington and Cunningham) shows that nowhere is reading aloud more important than in the first grade when students are just beginning to understand "talk written down."

Although this book is set up very much like the others—discrete assignments each consisting of a short reading passage, a letter to the parent, questions to be answered—there is a key difference. Because they are aimed at beginning readers, these selections are arranged sequentially (not just topically), with skills and word lists building carefully upon one another. Many of the language arts benchmarks are the same as those addressed in the other two books, but again, because this book is for beginning readers, each of its lessons is far more structured. My hope is that these homework assignments can meet a variety of needs—from those of any beginning reader to those of older, struggling readers, as well as adults who may be learning English as a second language.

Why Silent Reading Isn't Enough

As beginning readers build their skills, their teachers are tempted to allow them to complete more and more reading assignments with silent reading. Yes, sustained silent reading is highly effective in developing students' reading ability and increasing their motivation, and yes, children learn to read by reading—but beware! Often, while young students *appear* quite fluent as they're reading silently, they are not reading effectively, and their comprehension is poor. In fact, they often fail to use many of the word attack and comprehension skills we have tried to teach them.

Following is a list of the major pitfalls and shortcomings of silent reading:

○ Silent reading allows students to read quickly, often causing them to miss the main idea of the passage.

○ Silent reading allows students to skip words they do not know. Skipping unfamiliar words is often taught as a good reading strategy, and indeed it is. But it is only a good strategy if the student rereads the sentence and tries to figure out the unknown word through context or syntactic clues. We cannot tell if children reread for meaning when they are reading silently. We suspect that the good readers do reread, but the poorer readers, who need it the most, often do not.

○ Silent reading allows children to mispronounce words, which hampers their comprehension. Students may not recognize words in print that would sound familiar if they were read out loud.

○ Silent reading does not teach children to read with expression, to use voice inflections, or to adjust the rate of reading to reflect the content. Thus, they miss out on a great deal, such as the excitement of a story as it builds to a climax.

○ Silent reading offers teachers no information about the child's awareness of punctuation. On their own, many beginning readers just go along calling out words without pauses for periods or attention to quotation marks.

○ Silent reading does not encourage children to listen to themselves as they read, a habit that helps them to correct their errors and to insure that what they read makes sense.

Classroom Strategies for Maximizing Read-Aloud Experiences

While the subject of this book is increasing your students' oral reading skills through at-home work, let's first take a quick look at a few effective classroom strategies also aimed at augmenting read-aloud time. The two approaches—in-class reading and out-of-class reading—are merely different arenas for meeting the same instructional goals. The three classroom reading strategies described below avoid "round-robin" reading and are nonthreatening to poor readers.

1. **Read old favorites.** As the year progresses, go back and reread stories that have become familiar to children and thus are much easier to handle. Because they will feel more comfortable with the text, struggling readers are less likely to be embarrassed when called upon to read. And all students get more out of a story the second time through. Rereading old favorites thus helps to increase everyone's enjoyment of reading.

2. **Choral reading.** This is a particularly effective strategy for reading poetry, but for beginning readers, it is a good strategy in any genre. Reading aloud in a

group allows children to say the words they know and to listen to the group for help on the unfamiliar ones. Remember to read choral passages more than one time so that the unfamiliar words become familiar.

3. **Paired reading.** In this technique, students in pairs or groups of three are scattered around the classroom. Within each group, individuals take turns either reading whole stories or trading off with each new page. First graders approach this activity as a game. They like to listen to their friends and are ready helpers when someone is stuck on a word.

Easy-to-Use Homework Routine

As described earlier, the series of homework assignments in this book addresses the need for more oral reading practice and capitalizes on the enthusiasm of parents. Each week students receive a short passage to read aloud to their parents or caregivers. Then they answer a few related questions. The parents receive a letter designed to guide them through the reading and subsequent questions. Finally, both parent and child sign the homework page, indicating that they worked together on the assignment.

Because this book has been created for Grade 1, the stories are arranged in order of difficulty. Each story contains words from previous stories, plus some new ones.* Many of the skills practiced in the front of the book are repeated at a more difficult level later in the book. The relevant skill for the lesson is

Benefits of This Routine for Teachers, Parents, and Beginning Readers

Teachers everywhere are looking for simple ways to make their teaching lives easier while maintaining high-quality instruction. They want homework that is easily graded, yet meaningful to the child and relevant to the curriculum. Teachers need to find homework assignments that will help them reinforce mandated state assessment benchmarks, but they often must scramble to do so.

Parents everywhere appreciate homework that they understand, that reinforces concepts being taught in school, that is easy to complete, and that is sensitive to their busy schedules. They want to be reassured that the work their child is doing is meaningful to their child and relevant to the local curriculum and state assessment standards.

Beginning readers are usually excited about their new reading skills. They are anxious to practice them and proud to show off what they can do. This book capitalizes on their enthusiasm and gives them their moment in the spotlight every week.

In the introduction for each chapter, a chart identifies the number of new words for each selection, as well as the total number of words in the passage. (The same information is provided, on a per-lesson basis, in the top left corner of each lesson's first page.) I have based my identification of "new words" on years of observations from my own classroom instruction and my students' experiences. Nonetheless, we have chosen not to boldface or otherwise highlight particular new words within each selection, because these may in fact be known words to your own students and might thus prove confusing to readers. However, to provide you with as much background as possible, we include a list of the new words

at the end of each Skill Focus note within a chapter's introduction.

A few other points about my criteria in identifying new words: I did not count place or person names as new words. Nor did I count regular variations as new words. (That is, if students already knew the word look *and the story used the word* looked, *I did not count* looked *as new.) I did, however, distinguish between variations when the past tense of a verb was irregular. So, for example, the words* run *and* ran *are each considered new words. And note also that the stories with a large number of new words (for example, 15–19 new words) are always stories with lots of visual clues.*

highlighted at the top of the right-hand page of each lesson. Note that the story titles are purposely lower-cased in the first half of the book for readability. There are 31 story selections in the chapters themselves and three additional "bonus" poetry assignments in the Appendix. The intention is to provide you with enough homework lessons to span the entire school year. Brief explanations of the standards are included in the chapter introductions. Sample answers are on pages 94–96.

Here are some advantages to using this system:

○ **Children have ample time to complete the assignment.** Giving students an entire school week to turn in the homework removes a great deal of pressure from busy families. Many parents find that they are more likely to help with the work if it can be done at their own convenience.

○ **There is no expense involved.** Unlike many other parent projects that require expensive purchases, training nights, make-and-take games, and follow-up charts, this project gets all the parents involved at virtually no cost.

○ **Parents become aware of their child's reading ability.** When children first begin to read, it is a very exciting time—for parents *and* students! Parents love the work you are doing with their child and are very anxious to help out at home.

○ **The skills practiced are correlated to national reading standards.** Parents become aware of the skills that will eventually be tested on state and national exams in the higher grades. And teachers can look at these standards to make sure they are covering everything that is expected of them.

Reading Standards Addressed in This Book

The student . . .

determines the main idea of the text.

arranges events in chronological order.

uses context clues.

makes predictions before and during reading.

makes inferences and draws conclusions from story elements.

clarifies understanding by reading and self-correction.

recognizes when the author has used cause and effect.

summarizes the events of a story.

recognizes verb stems and suffixes and knows how suffixes change the meaning of a verb.

practices simple factual recall of text information.

practices phonics rules such as /ē/ ("long e").

learns to read compound words.

recognizes the author's use of compare and contrast.

understands how punctuation works in conversation.

recognizes antonyms.

practices alphabetical order.

recognizes story structure.

- **Students get credit, but not a grade, for returning the signed homework page.** This low-pressure evaluation means that you can quickly scan the returned pages and give "credit" or "no credit" marks, enabling you to focus on the far more important job of giving positive feedback to both parents and students. Mark the papers with comments, smiles, stars, or stickers to encourage both parents and children to continue with the work. Do not display a chart in the classroom indicating which students have returned their homework. This is very discouraging for those whose families will not or cannot help them. Evaluations should be private information in your grade book.

- **The assignments are instant homework.** Instead of having to hunt for or create meaningful assignments correlated with your curriculum, you can simply reproduce these standards-based activities.

- **The homework encourages communication between parents and teacher.** Parents receive a letter from you every week, helping them feel connected to what's going on in their child's classroom.

Hints for Success

Following is a list of guidelines to help you implement this homework routine:

- Pass out these homework assignments on the same day each week. (Mine go home on Mondays.)

- Allow until the end of the week to complete the work. (My students are allowed to turn in work any day up to and including Friday.)

- Insist that both the parent and the child sign at the top of the page.

- Make exceptions when needed. (I had one parent who worked nights through the week. I chose to accept her child's homework on Mondays so that she could help him over the weekend.) The main points are that the assignment is considered important and that it is done correctly.

- Assign homework "behind your teaching." This means that when you pass out a homework assignment, it should cover a skill that you have already taught. If you assign homework on a skill that you only introduced earlier that day, students may feel frustrated at home because neither they nor their parents quite know how to do the work. If you assign something that the child already understands, the homework will go much more smoothly. Generally speaking, homework should be a review or practice of skills already learned. Parents should not be expected to do the teaching at home.

- Introduce the homework routine with a letter like the one on page 10.

Dear Parents,

Welcome to the wonderful world of first grade! I know that you are anxious to help your child take those first steps to becoming a fluent reader. To help you do this, I will be sending home weekly reading assignments. This is a parent-child project that your child cannot do alone. Here's how it all works:

Each _____ your child will have a short reading homework assignment that asks you to listen to him or her read out loud at home.

The homework lesson includes a note to you each week that explains the assignment, to better help you to help your child. Please read it carefully.

After your child reads aloud, help him or her answer the questions at the bottom of the page. At the beginning of the year, you may have to do all of the writing, but as the year progresses, gradually encourage your child to do more and more of the work.

Sign at the top of the page. Your signature indicates that you listened to your child read and that you helped with the questions.

Return the paper to school. All homework assignments are due to me by _____ .

This simple project has been shown to improve reading fluency and comprehension. With your help, I feel that it can have great benefits for every child in my class. Please contact me if you have any questions concerning this project.

The first lesson is attached to this note and is due back by _____ . Thanks for all your help in getting your child off to a terrific start in becoming a great reader!

Sincerely,

Your child's teacher

Chapter 1

Sam the Cat

Passage	Skill Focus	Word Count—New Words
Sam	Factual recall	24—9
Sam will play	Making inferences from text	35—8
Sam is in	Identifying the /ē/ sound	30—4
Something new	Changing voice inflection; using question/ exclamation marks	34—4
Sam and a toy	Using context (text and visual) clues	39—6
Sam cannot play	Reading compound words	39—6

nlike older children, first-grade students are usually excited about having homework. They are anxious to show off their new reading skills to parents, grandparents, older siblings, neighbors, or anyone who will listen. Before you begin sending home this series of assignments, make sure that the students are able to read at this level. You do not want children (or their parents!) to experience frustration with beginning reading.

These first six stories are about a cat named Sam. They are intended to help children acquaint themselves with basic skills such as recalling events, looking at ending punctuation, and simple phonics.

Sam

◎ Skill Focus: Factual Recall

This simple story is a good way to launch beginning readers. It is very repetitious—and repetition, we know, builds word recognition and fluency. When evaluating this assignment, look for correct spelling of all of the words and capitalization of Sam's name. You may or may not choose to "take off" for errors, but at least make a notation for the student that he or she needs to pay attention to the spellings and the capitalization of Sam's name.

New Words: is, can, play, run, sleep, eat, jump, good, cat

Related Lessons

See additional lessons on Factual Recall in "Scruffy will ride" on page 40, and "After the Rain" on page 72.

Sam will play

◎ Skill Focus: Making Inferences From Text

The skill of drawing inferences and making assumptions from text is not easy for many beginning readers. Thus, as with all these homework assignments, be certain that you have introduced and taught the skill first in class so that the homework is truly practice. It's important, also, to make sure that students recognize all the words in this passage before you send it home as an assignment. This allows children to "show off" what they can do and get lots of positive feedback from parents. The more positive feedback they get, the more likely they are to repeat the action—which is exactly what we want them to do!

New Words: likes, to, he, will, go, up, look, down

Sam is in

◎ Skill Focus: Identifying the /ē/ Sound

The parent letter for this assignment describes a valuable technique for helping children use illustration clues in tandem with their knowledge of phonics when they encounter unknown words. By using this technique before asking a child to read a passage, you—or the parents—have not only prepared the child for a difficult word, but you've also made it easy for him or her to be successful. These kinds of activities make reading more fun for children, and when they're having fun, they're more likely to continue reading. But keep in mind that you'll need to assist children many times before this strategy becomes a habit for them.

New Words: in, here, out, it

Something new

◎ Skill Focus: Changing Voice Inflection; Using Question/Exclamation Marks

Most teachers automatically exaggerate their voice inflections when they are reading out loud to children because it helps young listeners to understand the plot, the emotions, and the action of the story. Beginning readers may not realize that literacy-related devices such as ending punctuation and illustrations—as well as our own prior knowledge concerning the story line—tell us when to change our voices. You can help your students understand inflection changes by providing instruction based on your own reading and on the kinds of cues mentioned above. One effective, fun way for students to practice different voice inflections is to have them read the same sentence using different ending punctuation. For example: "Did those children shout?" versus "Did those children shout!"

New Words: something, new, what, do

Sam and a toy

Skill Focus: Using Context (Text and Visual) Clues

You may want to prepare students for this homework lesson by doing the following classroom activity. Write the story below on the chalkboard. Then help students make a list of exclamatory phrases that would make sense for the blank space. Choose one and write it on the blank line. Then reread the story one or two more times.

> *STORY:* Sam will run. He will run to the mud. He will go in. Sam will go in the mud. _____ Sam is dirty. (Suggested phrases for the blank: "Oh, no!" "Bad, Sam!" "Look out!" "Don't, Sam!") Allow students to draw an illustration of Sam and a mud puddle. Then encourage them to write one of the phrases and the words, "Sam is dirty."

New Words: see, toy, with, the, and, not

> *Related Lesson*
>
> See additional lesson on Using Context Clues in "Who Is Out at Night?" on page 80.

Sam cannot play

Skill Focus: Reading Compound Words

Start a compound word chart, post it in your classroom, and put *something* and *cannot* (the two compound words in this story) at the top of the list. Whenever a student comes across a compound word in his or her reading, allow the child to copy that word onto the chart. Your chart will get really long in no time! Occasionally, review the chart and have students read all of the words. You can use the following strategy to help your students learn the compound words: For each compound, make a line to separate the two basic words.

New Words: at, does, cannot, get, help, now

> *Related Lesson*
>
> See additional lesson on Reading Compound Words in "The Moon" on page 79.

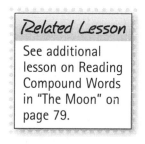

Parents, For Your Information: 24 words, 9 new words—
is, can, play, run, sleep, eat, jump, good, cat

LISTEN to your
child read this
story aloud.

Sam

Sam is a cat.
Sam can play.
Sam can run.

Sam can sleep.

Sam can eat.
Sam can jump.
Sam is a good cat.

Dear Parents,

One of the ways you can help a beginning reader is to teach him or her to look at the illustrations for clues about the story and any unfamiliar words. By teaching children to look carefully at the pictures, you encourage them to pay more attention to the helpful details. Looking for details is a skill that will aid them in all aspects of reading, including factual recall. For example, in this little story, both the text and the pictures can aid your child in answering the second question below. Remember to discuss pictures and illustrations before and during reading.

We completed this assignment together.

_____

(Child's Signature)

_____

(Parent's Signature)

The Questions

Answer these questions together and write the answers on the lines.

1. What is the cat's name?

_____

2. What are three things the cat can do?

_____   _____   _____

3. What kind of cat is Sam?

_____

Parents, For Your Information: 35 words, 8 new words—
likes, to, he, will, go, up, look, down

LISTEN to your
child read this
story aloud.

Sam will play

Sam is a cat.
Sam likes to play.
He will go.
He will go up.

Sam will go up, up, up.
Sam will look down.

Sam will jump.
Sam will jump down.
Sam will run.

16

Week-by-Week Homework for Building Reading Comprehension and Fluency: Grade 1
SCHOLASTIC TEACHING RESOURCES

Dear Parents,

In this story the cat sees his reflection in a mirror. This fact is not directly stated in the story. While the illustrations help to convey this message, the child must make an inference in order to explain why the cat jumped down. Thus, the skill we are working on for this story is called "making inferences from text." Because inferences may vary, accept (and write down) almost any reasonable answer your child gives.

We completed this
assignment together.

_____

(Child's Signature)

_____

(Parent's Signature)

The Questions

Help your child write a one- or two-word answer for each question.

1. Where did Sam go? _____

_____

2. What did he see? _____

_____

3. Why did Sam jump down? _____

_____

LISTEN to your
child read this
story aloud.

Sam is in

Sam will go in here.
He is in. Sam likes to
go in. He will look out.

Sam likes it in here.
Sam will sleep. Sam
will sleep in here.

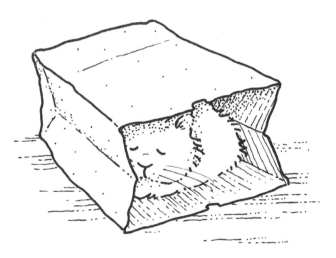

Week-by-Week Homework for Building Reading Comprehension and Fluency: Grade 1
SCHOLASTIC TEACHING RESOURCES

Dear Parents,

Before your child begins to read this story, look at the illustrations and point to the picture of the sleeping cat. Ask your child what the cat is doing. Then ask what sounds he or she can hear in the word sleep. Your child will probably respond, /s/, /sl/, or /ē/. Next ask your child to find a word in the story that has some of those sounds. With your child, circle or underline the word sleep so it will be easy to read (the sounds will be familiar) when he or she gets to that point of the story. This is a great technique to use for far more difficult words in more advanced reading.

We completed this
assignment together.

_____

(Child's Signature)

_____

(Parent's Signature)

The Questions

✳ • ✳

Go on a "long-e" hunt. Many of the words in this story have a "long e." That means that you say the name of the letter e when you say the word. Below, write all of the "long-e" words in the story (be sure to *write* a "long-e" word *every* time it appears in the story):

_____   _____

_____   _____

_____   _____

_____

Bonus: Which word has an e that is not the long sound? _____

LISTEN to your
child read this
story aloud.

Something new

Sam will go out.
Sam will run. It is
something new.
He will go up.

Sam will look down.
What will Sam do?
Sam will jump.

He will jump down.
LOOK! Sam will RUN!

Week-by-Week Homework for Building Reading Comprehension and Fluency: Grade 1
SCHOLASTIC TEACHING RESOURCES

Dear Parents,

As your child reads this story out loud to you, listen carefully for any voice inflections. The voice should go up slightly when there is a question and should show some excitement when there is an exclamation mark. Attention to changes in voice inflection and to punctuation are evidence of comprehension of the story line. If your child does not notice these things at first, try reading the story together. As you read together, make the appropriate changes in your own voice. Then see if you child will imitate you as you read through the story a third time.

We completed this
assignment together.

_____
(Child's Signature)

_____
(Parent's Signature)

The Questions

Using a red crayon or marker, help your child add the correct ending punctuation to the following sentences:

Sam will go to the water

What will Sam do

Sam will see a cat

Sam is scared

Will Sam look down

Sam will run and run and run

Parents, For Your Information: 39 words, 6 new words—
see, toy, with, the, and, not

LISTEN to your
child read this
story aloud.

Sam and a toy

Sam will see a toy.
It is a new toy. He will run.
He will play with the toy.
Sam will jump and play.
He will play and play.

_____!
It is not a good toy.

Sam will run.

Week-by-Week Homework for Building Reading Comprehension and Fluency: Grade 1
SCHOLASTIC TEACHING RESOURCES

Dear Parents,

Even if your child can read well, have him or her read every passage more than one time. Have your child read to grandparents, neighbors, siblings—anyone who will listen. This repetition will help build confidence as well as fluency and sight word recognition. The basic words in these stories are the basis for a great part of our language and should be recognized automatically.

This lesson centers on using context clues, both textual and visual. Have your child study the illustrations in order to suggest appropriate words that would make sense in the blank space. It is important for him or her to see the connection between the action described by the word(s) and the action shown in the illustration.

Using Context
(Text and Visual) Clues

We completed this
assignment together.

_____
(Child's Signature)

_____
(Parent's Signature)

The Questions

❋ • • • • • • • • • • • • • • • • ❋

Ask your child to point to the blank space in the story. Help him or her list at least five different words or two different word phrases for that space that might make sense in the story. Write the choices below; then write one of them on the blank line in the story. Have your child read the story one more time.

_____   _____

_____   _____

_____

Parents, For Your Information: 39 words, 6 new words—
at, does, cannot, get, help, now

LISTEN to your child read this story aloud.

Sam cannot play

Look at Sam. It is something new. Sam does not like it. He does not like something new.

Sam cannot play with something new. He will run. He will get help.

Look at Sam now. Now he can play.

Week-by-Week Homework for Building Reading Comprehension and Fluency: Grade 1
SCHOLASTIC TEACHING RESOURCES

Dear Parents,

This homework assignment deals with compound words. A compound word is made by putting two smaller words together to make one larger word. We use compound words all the time, usually without even realizing it. (In fact, the word **homework** itself is a great example!) Your child, no doubt, has already learned to use compound words in conversation.

Compound words often look frightening to children because they are so large! Help your child to realize that a compound word is really just two small words put together. You can do this by covering one half of the compound word at a time, first one side and then the other. After your child reads aloud each half, make sure he or she then reads aloud the one big word with no separation between the parts of the compound.

We completed this assignment together.

_____

(Child's Signature)

_____

(Parent's Signature)

The Questions

❋ • ❋

This story has two compound words. Write them here:

_____ _____

Have your mom or dad help you think of three more compound words. Write them here.

_____ _____

_____

(Mom and Dad—You can help with spelling or you can do the printing yourself.)

Sam and Scruffy

Passage	Skill Focus	Word Count—New Words
Scruffy is a dog	Comparing and contrasting	56—4
Sam wants to play	Sequencing events	67—3
Sam is sad	Summarizing	67—5
Sam is up	Identifying antonyms	67—3
Scruffy will help Sam	Creating mental images (visualizing)	59—2
Scruffy will ride	Factual recall; self-correction	78—7
A new toy for Sam and Scruffy	Identifying the *th* digraph	95—7
Untitled	Determining the main idea	86—6
Scruffy is in the house	Reading conversation/ dialogue	87—8

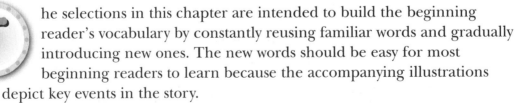

he selections in this chapter are intended to build the beginning reader's vocabulary by constantly reusing familiar words and gradually introducing new ones. The new words should be easy for most beginning readers to learn because the accompanying illustrations depict key events in the story.

This chapter's series of stories continue to feature Sam the cat, but they now include his new friend, a dog named Scruffy. The skill lessons are actually quite sophisticated—they include summarizing, comparing and contrasting, and sequencing events. But because they are presented within the context of these most basic beginning stories, they should be quite manageable for most of your students. The skills are presented here to begin laying a firm foundation for far more difficult reading and the challenges that students will encounter in future grades.

Week-by-Week Homework for Building Reading Comprehension and Fluency: Grade 1
SCHOLASTIC TEACHING RESOURCES

Scruffy is a dog

Skill Focus: Comparing and Contrasting

Comparing and contrasting is a basic literary convention. Keep in mind that many students in first grade need to learn the meanings of the words *compare* and *contrast,* as well as the underlying concepts, before they can recognize and interpret an author's use of this text pattern in something they've read. So, teaching the words and concepts may be your first priority here. From there, you can help your students recognize the use of this convention by repeating this lesson's activity each time students read a passage with a compare and contrast text pattern. Try not to belabor the point or make it a long, drawn-out lesson. After reading a story, simply ask how the characters were the same and how they were different.

New Words: dog, are, friends, bath

Sam wants to play

Skill Focus: Sequencing Events

There are several ways to teach sequencing. In addition to having students recall the correct chronological order of events in a story, you can ask them to recall events of their whole school day, the lunch period, recess time, or an art activity. Doing so helps to make this skill part of their real lives. As children describe events in chronological order, write them on chart paper. Then review the list to make sure this is the way that the events actually happened.

New Words: they, stop, around

Sam is sad

Skill Focus: Summarizing

This is by far the most difficult homework activity so far in this book. Children hate to leave things out, so instead of summarizing, they will think it necessary to put in every detail about the animals playing together and Sam's search for Scruffy. Be lenient when you are "grading" these assignments. And be aware that many parents will also have difficulty with this skill. If a number of your students (and their parents) do have difficulty with this assignment, ask students to copy the sample answer provided on page 94 and send the lesson back so that parents and children can discuss it. Remember, you will need to teach this difficult skill many times during the school year. The defining characteristic of a summary is actually quite simple—the details have been left out!

New Words: away, sad, for, no, happy

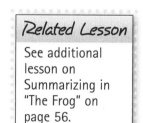

Related Lesson

See additional lesson on Summarizing in "The Frog" on page 56.

Sam is up

Skill Focus: Identifying Antonyms

Got five minutes before lunch or recess? Play the antonym game. You say a word and have the class or individuals respond with a word that means the opposite. Repeat this activity often, trying to elicit increasingly sophisticated words as the school year progresses. This is a wonderful activity for building vocabulary, even if some of the students wind up just listening. Following is a list of samples you might start with. (Student answers may vary but should convey an opposite or truly differing meaning from the given word.)

big—*little*; **large**—*small*; **enormous**—*tiny*; **good**—*bad*; **wonderful**—*terrible*; **super**—*awful*; **open**—*shut* or *closed*; **on**—*off*; **clean**—*dirty*; **spotless**—*filthy*; **hard**—*soft*; **hard**—*easy*; **long**—*short*; **broken**—*fixed*

New Words: wants, come, are

> ### Related Lessons
> See additional lessons on Identifying Antonyms in "The Rabbit and the Turtle" on page 58, and "Potatoes" on page 84.

Scruffy will help Sam

Skill Focus: Creating Mental Images (Visualizing)

For this lesson, evaluate the completed illustration based on the details suggested by the text and not on the quality of the child's drawing ability. If it is obvious to you that the parent has done the illustrating, write a short note reminding the parent that this goes beyond the role you would like him or her to play. Parents are to provide verbal suggestions and they may help with the writing down of the answers, but any creative or imaginative work should be the child's own. Figuring out how to help with homework (and not simply jumping in and doing it) may be quite a new challenge for some parents.

New words: rain, let

Scruffy will ride

Skill Focus: Factual Recall; Self-Correction

The questions that go with this story ask for factual recall, but they also ask the child to look at how the plot was developed in this story. ("Plot" is a relative term here! There certainly isn't much of it, but just enough for a first-grade story line.) It is important for the beginning reader to retell the plot—both orally and in writing—because the retelling lets us know that he or she did, indeed, understand what happened in the story and was monitoring his or her own reading. Do not underestimate the importance of this means of evaluation. Many students simply "word call," sometimes very convincingly, without ever understanding what they have read.

New Words: ride, fast, feel, wind, all, day, back

> ### Related Lessons
> See additional lessons on Factual Recall in "Sam" on page 14, and "After the Rain" on page 72.

A new toy for Sam and Scruffy

Skill Focus: Identifying the *th* Digraph

Write the *th* digraph at the top of a sheet of chart paper and include several familiar words (for example, *the* and *this*) that contain this digraph. Display the chart for your class. See if students can think of other words that begin this same way and add those words to the chart. As students continue to learn new words that have the /th/ sound, expand your chart to three columns so that you can list words with *th* in the initial, medial, and ending positions.

Consider creating additional charts for other digraphs or blends (for example, digraphs such as *ch* and *sh* and blends such as *bl, cl,* or *br*). (Remember, consonant digraphs are letter combinations that represent sounds not associated with either of the component parts, while in consonant blends, each individual sound retains its identity.) Encourage students to add words to the chart as they learn them or as they find them in their stories. Allowing children to do the writing gives them ownership in the project and makes them more apt to continue looking for words to add.

New Words: house, then, this, there, noise, too, again

Untitled

Skill Focus: Determining the Main Idea

As many as 40 percent of the questions on standardized reading tests may focus on the main idea of given passages. Since the main idea is usually reflected in the title, finding a title for a story (this lesson's activity) helps students to discern the main thing that happened in the story. In addition to using title-finding activities such as this, be sure to ask "main idea" questions frequently as your students read both fiction and nonfiction pieces in their daily work.

New Words: has, after, dig, hide, his, food

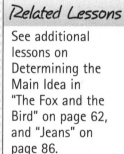

Related Lessons

See additional lessons on Determining the Main Idea in "The Fox and the Bird" on page 62, and "Jeans" on page 86.

Scruffy is in the house

Skill Focus: Reading Conversation/Dialogue

In this lesson, the suggestion for parents is to take turns reading with children. The parent might read the dialogue spoken by one character and the child might read the dialogue of the other. Try this in your classroom, too. You can read one part and have the students read the other (this is a good example of choral reading, which is also mentioned on page 77). Or, divide the class in half and let each side read the dialogue of the characters while you read the narrative parts between bits of dialogue. These variations in reading methods are fun for students and keep their attention focused.

New Words: bark, bow-wow, says, me, meow, loud, be, outside

Parents, For Your Information: 56 words, 4 new words—
dog, are, friends, bath

Scruffy is a dog

Scruffy is a dog.
Scruffy will run with Sam.

Scruffy will eat with Sam.
Scruffy will play with Sam.

Scruffy will sleep with
Sam. Scruffy and Sam
are friends. Scruffy will
get something new.

Scruffy will get a
bath. Sam will not
get a bath. Sam will
run. He will not get a
bath with Scruffy.

Week-by-Week Homework for Building Reading Comprehension and Fluency: Grade 1
SCHOLASTIC TEACHING RESOURCES

Dear Parents,

Recognizing when an author has used compare and contrast in a story or essay is an important literacy skill. Your child will need to know how to interpret this text pattern as he or she reads increasingly more complex fiction and nonfiction. You can help teach this skill by having your child compare Sam and Scruffy. How are they alike and how are they different? These are the two basic concepts in any comparing and contrasting activity—likeness and difference. Have fun with this activity!

Skill

Comparing and Contrasting

We completed this
assignment together.

_____

(Child's Signature)

_____

(Parent's Signature)

The Questions

Read these questions to your child and help him or her write the answers.

1. What do Sam and Scruffy do that is the same?

_____

_____

_____

2. What does Scruffy do that Sam does not do?

_____

_____

_____

Parents, For Your Information: 67 words, 3 new words—
they, stop, around

LISTEN to your child read this story aloud.

Sam wants to play

Sam and Scruffy are friends. They will run. They will play. Scruffy will stop. Sam will not stop. Sam will go up. He will go down.

Sam will play with Scruffy. Scruffy will not play with Sam. Sam will go around and around. He will go in and out. Scruffy will look at Sam.

Scruffy will go in. He will not play with Sam. Sam will sleep.

Week-by-Week Homework for Building Reading Comprehension and Fluency: Grade 1
SCHOLASTIC TEACHING RESOURCES

Dear Parents,

We may think that students can easily retell events in chronological order, but that is quite often not the case. Remember to ask your child to tell you what happened at school, at Grandma's, or at a birthday party and see if he or she can recount the events in the correct order. You can help your child become a better reader by having him or her recall facts or events in the order in which they occurred.

We completed this assignment together.

_____

(Child's Signature)

_____

(Parent's Signature)

The Questions

Help your child read this question and write one- or two-word answers. What are all the things that Sam does? Write them in the correct order.

1. _____

2. _____

3. _____

4. _____

5. _____

6. _____

7. _____

LISTEN to your
child read this
story aloud.

Sam is sad

Sam and Scruffy will play and play. Scruffy will stop. He will run. He will run away to something new. Sam is sad. Sam will not play. Sam will not eat.

Sam will look for Scruffy. He will look up. He will look down. He will look in and out. No Scruffy.

Now Sam is happy. Sam will play. Sam will eat. Sam and Scruffy will sleep.

Dear Parents,

This activity asks your child to summarize the story. Help him or her learn how to do this by asking for a retelling of the story in one sentence. Provide this hint: "You can leave out the part where Sam and Scruffy play at the beginning and at the end of the story. Look at the illustrations to help you find three main events." Accurately summarizing the events may take some practice, and it may take your child a few tries. You might want to write the sentences on a piece of scrap paper before copying the final version onto the answer section of this homework page.

We completed this assignment together.

_____
(Child's Signature)

_____
(Parent's Signature)

The Questions

✳ • ✳

Write one sentence that tells what happened in this story.

_____

_____

_____

_____

LISTEN to your
child read this
story aloud.

Sam is up

Sam wants to go up. He will go up, up, up. He will look down. He will see Scruffy. Scruffy will not go up. Sam will not come down. They cannot play. They cannot eat. They are not happy. Sam and Scruffy are sad. Sam cannot come down.

Scruffy will get help. He will run and run.

Now Sam is down. Now Sam and Scruffy can play.

Week-by-Week Homework for Building Reading Comprehension and Fluency: Grade 1
SCHOLASTIC TEACHING RESOURCES

Dear Parents,

Antonyms are two words that have opposite meanings, like on and off. In this homework assignment, your child is going to find the pairs of words that are antonyms. This should be an easy activity for your child, but if it is not, practice finding antonyms with him or her before tackling the assignment. Try saying the following words and see if your child can tell you the opposites. (You may have to help at first and you may need to run through more than the ones that are listed here.)

high—low; new—old; hot—cold; wet—dry; quiet—loud or noisy; sunny—cloudy or rainy or stormy

Skill
Identifying Antonyms

We completed this assignment together.

_____
(Child's Signature)

_____
(Parent's Signature)

The Questions

Write the word that means the opposite of each word. (Parents: You can help, but let the child do the writing for this one.)

up _____

will _____ _____ (**Hint:** Two words)

happy _____

play _____ _____ (**Hint:** Two words)

Now think of two other pairs of antonyms and write them here.

_____ _____

_____ _____

LISTEN to your
child read this
story aloud.

Scruffy will help Sam

Sam is out. He looks up. He sees rain. Sam cannot go in.

Sam will run. He will run and run. He will run to Scruffy. He does not like rain.

Scruffy will let him in. Sam and Scruffy are in. Sam and Scruffy look at the rain. They are happy now. They are not in the rain.

Week-by-Week Homework for Building Reading Comprehension and Fluency: Grade 1
SCHOLASTIC TEACHING RESOURCES

Dear Parents,

One way to measure young children's reading comprehension is to ask them to illustrate what they understand from the printed word. This homework activity asks your child to create a mental picture of what has happened in the story and then draw that picture on this page. Have your child read the story out loud at least two times. Then ask him or her to draw a picture of Sam and Scruffy at the end of the story. See if your child can do this independently, but you are welcome to suggest details if the activity becomes frustrating for him or her.

We completed this
assignment together.

_____

(Child's Signature)

_____

(Parent's Signature)

The Questions

Reread the last paragraph of the story. Discuss what happened. In the box below, draw a picture of the ending of the story. Where are Sam and Scruffy? How do they feel? What do they see?

Parents, For Your Information: 78 words, 7 new words—
ride, fast, feel, wind, all, day, back

LISTEN to your child read this story aloud.

Scruffy will ride

Sam will sleep. He will sleep and sleep.

Here comes Scruffy. He will get in.

Now Sam and Scruffy will ride. Scruffy likes to ride. He likes to go fast. He likes to feel the wind. He looks at Sam. Sam is not happy. He does not like to ride. He does not like to ride fast.

Sam will get out. He will jump down. Scruffy will ride and ride all day. Sam will go back to sleep.

Dear Parents,

Researchers have shown that reading drastically improves when students are asked to read out loud. If you hear your child make a reading error, do not jump immediately to correct it. Let him or her read to the end of the sentence or the end of the paragraph. If readers are listening to themselves read, they will be able to hear that what they said aloud did not make sense. Most students will automatically reread and self-correct their error. This is an important skill for children to acquire as they develop reading and comprehension skills, including the skill of factual recall, which is the focus of this lesson's activity.

We completed this assignment together.

_____
(Child's Signature)

_____
(Parent's Signature)

The Questions

* • *

Answer these questions together:

1. What was Sam doing at the start of the story? _____

2. What did Scruffy do? _____

_____

3. Why didn't Sam stay with Scruffy? _____

_____

4. What was Sam doing at the end of the story? _____

_____

5. Who do you think was pulling the wagon? _____

_____

Parents, For Your Information: 95 words, 7 new words—
house, then, this, there, noise, too, again

LISTEN to your
child read this
story aloud.

A new toy for
Sam and Scruffy

Sam and Scruffy are in the
house. They run and jump and
play. They like to go in the
house. Then Scruffy sees
something new. What is it? This
is a new toy.

Scruffy will play with the
toy. There is noise! Sam will
play too. There is no noise
now. Scruffy will play again.
There is noise. Sam will play
again. There is no noise.
What is this something new?

What toy is this? The
toy will go away.

Sam and Scruffy are not
in the house. They cannot
play with the new toy.

Week-by-Week Homework for Building Reading Comprehension and Fluency: Grade 1
SCHOLASTIC TEACHING RESOURCES

Dear Parents,

This story contains several words that may be confusing for your child. Can you see why? It is because three of the new words all begin with the same consonant digraph—the /th/ sound. When students are learning to read, they often form the habit of looking at just the beginning of words. This week's lesson is set up to make them look at the letters at the middle and at the end of each of the /th/ words. As you focus on these words, it will be helpful to point out that the word **they** has an /ā/ sound, even though it is spelled with an e. If this activity is difficult for your beginning reader, start by circling or highlighting all the **th** digraphs in the story.

Skill
Identifying the *th* Digraph

We completed this assignment together.

_____
(Child's Signature)

_____
(Parent's Signature)

The Questions

Go on a search for the /th/ sound! Look carefully at the story you just read. Now make a list of all of the different words that have the /th/ sound in them. (**Hint:** Sometimes the letters *th* and the /th/ sound come in the middle or at the end of a word!)

_____ _____ _____

_____ _____

_____ _____

Bonus: What was the new toy?

_____

LISTEN to your
child read this
story aloud.

What is this? Scruffy has something to eat. He will eat and eat and eat. Sam looks at Scruffy. He wants to eat too.

Scruffy will run. He will not let Sam eat. Sam will run. He runs after Scruffy. He wants to eat.

Sam looks at Scruffy. Scruffy will dig. He will dig and dig and dig. He will hide his food.

Now there is no food. Sam will go to the house.

He can eat there. There is food in the house for Sam.

Dear Parents,

One of the more difficult reading skills is figuring out the main idea of an article or story. After your child has read this story and looked at the illustrations, simply ask him or her to tell you what happened in the story. After this retelling, ask your child to think of a good title for the story. The title (especially of a simple story for this grade level) usually conveys the main idea. Thus, by creating a title, your child will be identifying the main idea of the story. Do not become discouraged if this activity seems difficult for your child. This skill lesson will be practiced again and again during your child's school years.

We completed this
assignment together.

_____

(Child's Signature)

_____

(Parent's Signature)

The Questions

Think of four good titles for this story. Write them all here.

_____

_____

_____

_____

Now choose your favorite title and write it on the line at the top of the story page.

Parents, For Your Information: 87 words, 8 new words—
bark, bow-wow, says, me, meow, loud, be, outside

LISTEN to your child read this story aloud.

Scruffy is in the house

Scruffy likes to play with Sam. He runs to Sam to play. Scruffy will bark. "Bow-wow," says Scruffy. "Come and play with me."

"Meow," says Sam. "I like to sleep."

Scruffy will run and bark. He will jump up and down. He will run in the house.

"Meow," says Sam. "I will sleep all day."

Scruffy jumps up. He looks down. Then there is noise. It is a loud noise. Sam cannot sleep!

Scruffy must go out. He cannot be in the house. He can play outside.

Dear Parents,

This story may be one of the first experiences your child has reading dialogue. There are several things that make this kind of reading difficult for children. They see numerous paragraphs, each with many commas and quotation marks. Also, the sentences are broken up with phrases like "said Sam." All of this can initially prove challenging to a beginning reader. Your child may need to read this story several times to understand the change in speakers. If he or she is still having difficulty, take turns reading—you read Sam's part and let your child read Scruffy's part, and then switch roles.

Skill
Reading Conversation/Dialogue

We completed this assignment together.

_____
(Child's Signature)

_____
(Parent's Signature)

The Questions

❋ • ❋

Write one thing that Sam says to Scruffy after he says "Meow." Don't forget to add quotation marks and ending punctuation.

"Meow," says Sam. _____

_____

Write what Scruffy says to Sam after he says "Bow-wow." Don't forget to add quotation marks and ending punctuation.

"Bow-wow," says Scruffy. _____

_____

Week-by-Week Homework for Building Reading Comprehension and Fluency: Grade 1
SCHOLASTIC TEACHING RESOURCES

47

Fables and Folk Tales

Passage	Skill Focus	Word Count—New Words
The Lion and the Mouse	Recognizing cause and effect	116—14
A Girl in the Woods	Forming past tense	104—15
The Frog	Summarizing	109—16
The Rabbit and the Turtle	Identifying antonyms	136—13
A Boy and His Trick	Identifying story patterns	154—16
The Fox and the Bird	Determining the main idea	137—13
The Mice and the Cat	Alphabetizing words	132—14

n the following selections you will find several familiar fables and folk tales, each of which has been carefully rewritten so that beginning readers can read them independently. The stories are, by necessity, very much simplified and even the titles are new, but you will certainly recognize all of the stories here. Reading the picture-book version of each story out loud would make a good follow-up activity with these lessons.

Some of the skills in this chapter are fundamental reading skills such as recognizing cause and effect or determining the main idea. Others, such as putting words in alphabetical order and using past tense verbs correctly, are key grammar skills. All of the skill lessons have been simplified in order to be manageable for the youngest learners.

The Lion and the Mouse

Skill Focus: Recognizing Cause and Effect

The cause-and-effect pattern within a text is a challenging one for students to identify. You can help children grasp this text pattern more easily by focusing their attention first on the *effect*, rather than the cause, and working backward. Start with some classroom examples. For instance, you might ask, "Why was Tommy late for lunch?" or, "Why did the paint get spilled?" These questions focus on the effects, or results, of a prior action. Tommy had to go to the sink to wash his hands (the cause); thus, he was late for lunch (the effect). The paint was sitting on the edge of the sink (the cause); thus, it spilled (the effect). In this story, you might ask, "Why did the mouse help the lion?" One possible answer is "The mouse helped the lion (effect) because the lion had first helped him (cause)." Children usually have an easier time explaining and understanding causes if they know what the effects were.

New Words: once, was, lion, mouse, ran, said, you, my, supper, someday, little, rope, chewed, but

A Girl in the Woods

Skill Focus: Forming Past Tense

This lesson makes you wonder why we even have rules in the English language. Although the rule for past tense verbs does actually operate much of the time, it often seems that almost everything is an exception to the rule! This story was constructed specifically to give students practice with irregular verbs, which of course do not follow the rule.

Young children will automatically apply a rule they know, even if they cannot yet verbalize it. For instance, they know we add *-ed* to words to indicate past tense. That is why you hear children say that they "swimmed" yesterday or "eated" this morning. At this stage, they are simply generalizing the rule to all words. To help your readers keep track of the irregular verbs they discover, consider making a classroom chart to list such words.

New Words: girl, she, woods, went, ate, some, sat, chair, slept, bed, three, bears, oh, on, stayed

The Frog

Skill Focus: Summarizing

Every time you read a story aloud to your class, you can teach this valuable skill. The key is to structure your questions so that when the answers are put together, they actually summarize the story. For instance, here is a set of questions you could use for *Miss Nelson is Missing* by James Marshall. This story features the infamous substitute, Viola Swamp. You might ask your students, "What were the children doing wrong? Who was the new teacher? How did the children act when Miss Nelson came back?" You might then instruct

> ### Related Lesson
> See additional lesson on Summarizing in "Sam is sad" on page 34.

them, "Now complete these sentences: The children were _____ and _____.
Then _____ _____ came to be the teacher. When Miss Nelson returned, the
children were _____."

Also, remember to use this activity with nonfiction stories as well as fiction, to
help your students learn to summarize both types of writing.

New Words: frog, pond, saw, big, father, give, him, kissed, handsome, prince, got,
married, lived, happily, ever, after

The Rabbit and the Turtle

Skill Focus: Identifying Antonyms

Being able to recognize both synonyms and antonyms is important for young
readers, but antonym identification is far easier to teach. Remember to play the
antonym game (page 28) informally and frequently in class.

Here's another way to teach antonyms: When you assign this story, take a few
minutes to have students brainstorm pairs of antonyms. Have students form groups
of three or four and give a sheet of paper to a "recorder" (the best speller or writer)
in each group. Set a timer for five minutes; in this time, each
group thinks of as many pairs of opposites as they can, and the
recorder writes them down. Afterward, have groups present their
lists to the class. Try not to focus on the numbers of antonym pairs
generated by each group. This activity should not be a
competition. Encourage students to add to their lists throughout
the day. This is important because some of the best antonym pairs
may come to students in other settings—for example, at lunch
(*good* and *yukky*) or on the playground (*high* and *low*).

> ### Related Lessons
> See additional
> lessons on
> Identifying
> Antonyms in "Sam
> is up" on page 36,
> and "Potatoes" on
> page 84.

New Words: rabbit, turtle, slow, did, one, want, race, yes, as, woke, won, lost, win

A Boy and His Trick

Skill Focus: Identifying Story Patterns

Many children's stories have a distinct story structure. For instance, many fables and
folk tales follow a pattern in which there are three events leading up to the climax of
the story. Help your students recognize this story structure by preselecting stories
built this way and reading them aloud to your class. (Besides this story, you might use
"The Three Little Pigs," "Goldilocks and the Three Bears," "Cinderella," or one of
the many fairy tales in which three wishes, events, or people are featured.) As the
school year progresses, continue to point out stories that follow this familiar pattern
of events and ultimately broaden the variety of story patterns and structures that you
expect children to recognize.

New Words: boy, tricks, field, take, care, sheep, town, called, wolf, people, scare,
laughed, just, next, real, of

The Fox and the Bird

Skill Focus: Determining the Main idea

In this lesson, as in several previous lessons, students are asked to determine the main idea of the story. Unlike those lessons, however, here the main idea is implied, rather than directly stated. Although you may be so familiar with the fable of the fox and the grapes that the lesson seems obvious, if you examine the story carefully, you'll note that there is no explicit statement about why the fox changed his mind and no longer wanted the grapes. (Since he couldn't reach them, he decided they were probably no good anyway.)

This may well be your students' first experience with drawing inferences from text, and therefore, it could prove a very difficult activity for some. When these papers are returned to school, look for a great variety of answers from your students and their parents and be lenient with "grading" the completed work. Count as correct any answers that make logical sense and that do not distort the original intent of the fable.

> **Related Lessons**
>
> See additional lessons on Determining the Main Idea in "Untitled" on page 44, and "Jeans" on page 86.

New Words: fox, grapes, I, would, missed, could, bird, came, fly, them, myself, probably, sour

The Mice and the Cat

Skill Focus: Alphabetizing Words

Alphabetizing is a skill children need to learn. The list in the Questions section for this lesson includes the names of all the animals that have been mentioned thus far in these homework assignments; students are asked to put these animal names in alphabetical order. This deceptively difficult task will no doubt take children some time to complete. Be sure your students have at least a basic understanding of alphabetical order before you send this assignment home. Otherwise, the lesson is certain to be frustrating and unpleasant for both children and their parents.

New Words: who, chased, were, afraid, had, an, idea, tie, bell, hear, us, mice, put, we

Parents, For Your Information: 116 words, 14 new words—once, was, lion, mouse, ran, said, you, my, supper, someday, little, rope, chewed, but

LISTEN to your child read this story aloud.

The Lion and the Mouse

Once there was a lion. He liked to sleep and eat. A mouse liked to run. He ran to the lion. The lion said, "Stop. I will eat you for my supper."

The mouse said, "No, no. Do not eat me. Someday I will help you."

"You cannot help me," said the lion. "You are too little to help me."

"You will see," said the mouse.

Then the lion was in a rope. The mouse ran to the lion. "I will help you now," said the mouse. The mouse chewed the rope.

The lion said, "You can help me, Mouse. You are little, but you can help a lion." Now the mouse and lion are friends.

Dear Parents,

Much of what we are doing with these easy reading passages is laying the groundwork for more sophisticated lessons. The story "The Lion and the Mouse" is a good example of this. This week's skill focus is recognizing the "cause-and-effect" text pattern; in upper grades, where reading passages are much more complex, this can be a challenging skill for students to master. Be sure to take a few minutes to talk to your child about events in this story. Your child should understand that because the lion was nice to the mouse, the mouse returned the favor and saved the lion's life.

We completed this
assignment together.

_____
(Child's Signature)

_____
(Parent's Signature)

The Questions

Answer these questions together.

1. How did the lion help the mouse?_____

_____

2. How did the mouse help the lion?_____

_____

3. Why did the mouse help the lion?_____

_____

4. What lesson can you learn from this story?_____

_____

Parents, For Your Information: 104 words, 15 new words—girl, she, woods, went, ate, some, sat, chair, slept, bed, three, bears, oh, on, stayed

LISTEN to your child read this story aloud.

A Girl in the Woods

Once there was a little girl. She ran into the woods. She ran to a house and went in. She ate some food. Then she sat in a chair. Then she slept in a bed. Three bears came to the house. They looked at the food. They saw the chair. Then they looked at the bed. The girl was in the little bed.

"Oh, no," said the girl.

"Oh, no," said the bears. "You ate the food. You sat on the chair. You slept in the bed."

The girl ran and ran. She ran to her house. She stayed in the house all day.

Dear Parents,

This story is told mainly in the past tense. That means that the events of the story already happened. This week's homework lesson asks your child to write the past tense verb—which appears in the story—next to the present tense verb for that same word. (The present tense verb should already be familiar to your child.) Verbs that are "regular" follow the rule for forming past tense: usually add -ed. But this story purposely contains only two such regular verbs. All of the rest are "irregular," which means that they do not follow the rule. (Example: run/ran, not runned.)

We completed this assignment together.

_____
(Child's Signature)

_____
(Parent's Signature)

The Questions

✳ • • • • • • • • • • • • • • • • • • • ✳

Look at the list of verbs (action words) below. Find a word in the story that is the past tense of each word. To get you started, we've provided an example of an irregular verb.

Regular Verbs (add -ed)

look _____

stay _____

Irregular Verbs (don't add -ed)

run __**ran**_____

see _____

go _____

eat _____

sleep _____

come _____

sit _____

say _____

Parents, For Your Information: 109 words, 16 new words—
frog, pond, saw, big, father, give, him, kissed, handsome,
prince, got, married, lived, happily, ever, after

LISTEN to your
child read this
story aloud.

The Frog

Once there was a frog in a pond. He jumped out and went in the woods. He jumped and jumped. He saw a house. It was a big house. A girl was there. She said, "Father, I see a frog. I will give him some food." The frog ate the food. He sat on a chair. He liked the girl. She liked the frog.

The girl and the frog liked to play. The girl kissed the frog. Now he was not a frog! He was a handsome prince. He and the girl got married. They lived happily ever after in the big house in the woods with the pond.

Week-by-Week Homework for Building Reading Comprehension and Fluency: Grade 1
SCHOLASTIC TEACHING RESOURCES

Dear Parents,

By now you've probably realized that many of the activities and skills are repeated in these homework assignments. That's because all key reading skills need to be taught several times and reviewed many times before a young reader will actually be able to make use of them independently.

This assignment asks your child to summarize a story. Summarizing is a lot like determining the main idea, but it is more comprehensive. When summarizing, you need to include **all** major events from the story. Before you and your child tackle the questions below, help him or her answer these questions:

1. Who did the frog go to see? _____
2. What did the girl do to the frog? _____
3. How does the story end? _____

We completed this assignment together.

_____
(Child's Signature)

_____
(Parent's Signature)

The Questions

Look at the answers to the questions above. Now use those answers below to write a two-sentence summary of the story. (**Hint:** The number of blank spaces tells you how many words fit there.)

One day a _____ went to see a _____ and

she _____ _____. They got _____

and lived _____ _____ _____.

LISTEN to your child read this story aloud.

The Rabbit and the Turtle

Once there was a rabbit and a turtle. The rabbit liked to run. He liked to run fast. The turtle was slow. He did not like to run. He did not like to go fast. One day the rabbit said, "Turtle, do you want to race?" "Yes," said the turtle. "I can go as fast as you." "No, you cannot," said the rabbit. "You are slow and I am fast."

The rabbit ran fast. The turtle was slow. The rabbit stopped and went to sleep. The turtle did not stop. He was slow, but he did not stop. He did not sleep.

The rabbit woke up. The turtle won the race. The rabbit lost. The rabbit was sad and the turtle was happy. "You are slow, Turtle, but you can win the race," said the rabbit.

Week-by-Week Homework for Building Reading Comprehension and Fluency: Grade 1
SCHOLASTIC TEACHING RESOURCES

Dear Parents,

This familiar story has been rewritten to emphasize the use of antonyms. Antonyms are two words that have opposite meanings, such as hot and cold, or long and short. Although we don't expect your child to know the word **antonym** yet, he or she should recognize antonyms in this story and be able to use them correctly in conversation. Try playing this game with your child. You say, "I think it is hot." The child replies, "I think it is cold." You say, "I think it is long." The child replies, "I think it is short." Continue in this manner, making this a fun, even nonsensical, game.

We completed this assignment together.

_____
(Child's Signature)

_____
(Parent's Signature)

The Questions

Use opposites to answer these two questions.

1. How did the turtle move? _____

2. How did the rabbit move? _____

Now find two more pairs of opposites in the story. (**Hint:** Both pairs are in the second paragraph.)

3. _____   _____

4. _____   _____

Parents, For Your Information: 154 words, 16 new words—
boy, tricks, field, take, care, sheep, town, called, wolf,
people, scare, laughed, just, next, real, of

LISTEN to your
child read this
story aloud.

A Boy and His Trick

Once there was a little boy who liked to play tricks.
He was to go to the field and take care of the sheep.

One day he ran to the town and called, "Wolf! Wolf!" The people in the town ran to the field to scare the wolf. The boy laughed. It was just his trick.

The next day the boy was in the field. He ran to the town and called, "Wolf! Wolf!" The people ran to the field to scare the wolf. The boy laughed. It was just his trick again.

The next day the boy was in the field with the sheep. A real wolf came to eat the sheep! The boy ran to the town and called, "Wolf! Wolf!" but the people did not come.

"It is just a trick," they said. The wolf ate all of the sheep and the boy was sad. He did not play tricks again.

Week-by-Week Homework for Building Reading Comprehension and Fluency: Grade 1
SCHOLASTIC TEACHING RESOURCES

Dear Parents,

Most adults recognize this familiar story structure. The same event happens two times, and then something unexpected and different happens with the third occurrence. Other examples of this pattern include stories like "The Three Little Pigs" and "The Three Bears." Jokes and riddles are also often structured this way. Beginning readers do not need to know that many stories they will come across in the future will take this same form, but they do need to recognize this story structure when they encounter it in their present reading. Help your child to answer the story pattern questions below.

We completed this assignment together.

_____

(Child's Signature)

_____

(Parent's Signature)

The Questions

✳ • • • • • • • • • • • • • • • • • ✳

Answer these questions together.

1. What happened the first time the boy called out "Wolf!"?

_____

2. What happened the second time the boy called out "Wolf!"?

_____

3. What happened the *third* time the boy called out "Wolf!"?

_____

4. Why didn't the people come the third time?

_____

5. What lesson can you learn from this story?

_____

Parents, For Your Information: 137 words, 13 new words—fox, grapes, I, would, missed, could, bird, came, fly, them, myself, probably, sour

LISTEN to your child read this story aloud.

The Fox and the Bird

Once there was a fox. He liked to eat. He saw some grapes. "I would like to eat the grapes," said the fox.

He jumped to get the grapes, but he missed. He jumped again and again, but he could not get the grapes. Then a bird came. The bird could fly and eat the grapes.

"The grapes are good," said the bird to the fox. "Do you want some grapes?"

"I can get the grapes," said the fox. "I can get them myself."

He jumped and jumped, but he could not get the grapes. The bird looked at the fox.

"What will you do now, Fox?"

"I do not want the grapes now," said the fox. "They are not good grapes. They are probably sour grapes."

And the fox went away, but he did not eat.

Dear Parents,

Several homework activities in this book ask your child to determine the main idea of a reading selection. We keep asking this because it is the basis for most comprehension questions and a popular question on standardized tests. The main idea in this particular story is somewhat difficult to identify because it is not directly stated. This means that the child has to "read between the lines" of the story. Your child may need some assistance with this difficult task. Try not to simply tell him or her the answer. Instead, do some careful questioning to see if your child can arrive at the right answer on his or her own. (**Hint:** Try reading the story more than one time.)

We completed this assignment together.

_____

(Child's Signature)

_____

(Parent's Signature)

The Questions

Answer these questions. The three answers together are the main idea of the story.

1. What did the fox want? _____

2. Why did he change his mind? _____

3. Why did the fox say the grapes were sour? _____

_____

Parents, For Your Information: 132 words, 14 new words—who, chased, were, afraid, had, an, idea, tie, bell, hear, us, mice, put, we

The Mice and the Cat

Once there was a mouse who lived in a house with a cat. But the cat was not his friend. The cat wanted to eat the mouse for food. The cat chased the mouse in the house.

The mouse went to his friends. They were afraid of the cat, too. One mouse had an idea. "Let's tie a bell on the cat," said the mouse. "Then we will hear him coming to chase us."

"That is a good idea," said the mice. "Would you do it? Would you put the bell on the cat?"

"No," said the mouse. "I will not go to the cat."

"No," said all of the mice. "We will not go to the cat. It is a good idea, but who will put the bell on the cat?"

Week-by-Week Homework for Building Reading Comprehension and Fluency: Grade 1
SCHOLASTIC TEACHING RESOURCES

Dear Parents,

Putting words into alphabetical order may appear to be a simple task, but it calls upon several kinds of knowledge. Please begin this activity by having your child repeat the alphabet a couple of times. Say it together to make it more fun. Now look at the list of animals below. Have your child underline the first letter of each animal name. Then, as you say the alphabet for the third time, pause after each letter and give your child time to search for an animal name that begins with that letter. Continue through the alphabet until your child has written all of the animal names on the lines. Finally, check the work by saying the alphabet again and, together, making sure that everything is in the correct place.

We completed this assignment together.

_____
(Child's Signature)

_____
(Parent's Signature)

The Questions

All of the homework stories so far have featured one of the animals listed below. Draw a red line under the first letter of each word. Now write their names in ABC order. Be careful to spell correctly. (**Hint:** Two words begin with the same letter.) The first one is done for you.

Animals: cat, dog, lion, mouse, bears, rabbit, turtle, wolf, fox, bird

1. bears 2. _____ 3. _____ 4. _____

5. _____ 6. _____ 7. _____

8. _____ 9. _____ 10. _____

Bonus: Why did the mice want to put a bell on the cat?

_____

What was the problem with this idea? _____

_____

Fiction and Nonfiction "Go-Togethers"

Passage	Skill Focus	Word Count—New Words
Sad Day, Happy Day	Adding endings to verbs	126—6
After the Rain	Factual recall	135—23
Roy G. Biv	Understanding acronyms	131—15
A Night Walk	Using quotation marks	136—7
The Moon	Reading compound words	150—12
Who Is Out at Night?	Using context clues	153—16
The Picnic	Identifying words with the letter *a*	149—10
Potatoes	Identifying antonyms	156—17
Jeans	Stating the main idea	136—17

 n the past, literacy educators believed that before the age of nine students "learn to read," and after age nine they "read to learn." This chapter is based on the premise that even the youngest students can "read to learn." That is why the following selections are presented as "go-together" groupings, each consisting of one fiction story followed by two nonfiction pieces. You may need to present some mini-lessons as you assign these selections to be sure that your students know the difference between fiction and nonfiction writing.

Several skills presented in previous chapters are repeated here in this last one. Students need a good deal of repetition before they recognize compound words or are able to add the correct endings to verbs. Remember, it's important to present these same skills in your daily mini-lessons or small-group instruction before assigning the homework so the learning is fresh in students' minds.

Sad Day, Happy Day

Skill Focus: Adding Endings to Verbs

Recognizing base words and endings helps students become better readers. At this early level, techniques as simple as this lesson's "sounding out" activity should help your students begin to grasp the concept of separating a base word from a suffix.

You can extend this activity by creating a chart with one column listing the basic verb forms, also called verb stems (for example, *pull*), and two columns for the suffixes *-ed* and *-ing*. Have students add these suffixes to the basic verb forms to create new words: under the *-ed* column students would write *pulled* and under the *-ing* column they would write *pulling*. Be sure to have every child add at least one word to the chart and ask him or her to use the word in a sentence. Students will come up with words that are exceptions to the rule *(run, running, but not runned)*. For those, you can create a separate chart and call it "Tricky Verbs."

New Words: their, sun, shine, still, made, rainbow

After the Rain

Skill Focus: Factual Recall

> *Related Lessons*
>
> See additional lessons on Factual Recall in "Sam" on page 14, and "Scruffy will ride" on page 72.

Questions that focus on factual recall are questions that require students to go back to the story to find the answer. When we use such questions, we need to make sure they are indeed a direct reflection of the actual text. This is the definition of a literal question. Correct answers should consist of exactly what is stated in the original text.

Do not expect beginning readers to evaluate, interpret, or otherwise manipulate information. They will have plenty of time to practice those skills as their reading comprehension improves.

New Words: dirt, may, earthworm, funny, have, arms, legs, bones, ears, nose, teeth, leaves, tunnel, move, rock, air, make, plants, grow, need, our, where, walk

Roy G. Biv

Skill Focus: Understanding Acronyms

In addition to weather-related rainbows, your students can also find rainbows in the arc of a garden hose's water or in soap bubbles. Make this reading assignment more fun by providing students the opportunity to discover one of these smaller rainbows (and Roy G. Biv) right in the classroom. Try doing this before you send home the assignment so that students will have built more background knowledge.

Remember that doing hands-on activities with your students not only clarifies the key concept for children but it also has a wonderful side effect. It makes children more excited about coming to school and makes reading nonfiction more appealing.

New Words: know, name, say, colors, always, must, same, time, your, sunlight, red, top, orange, guess, use

A Night Walk

🌀 **Skill Focus:** Using Quotation Marks

This activity provides a visual example of how quotation marks actually work on the page. Be sure to do the following three activities in your classroom before you send home this assignment:

Write a story on chart paper that consists of dialogue, but leave the quotation marks out. Have students come up and add green (opening) and red (closing) quotation marks around the dialogue.

Use a white-out marker to erase the quotation marks on a short story. Then have the class work as a whole group to add green and red quotation marks where appropriate.

Use the same activity as above, but this time, have students work independently to add back the quotation marks.

New Words: night, stars, moon, beautiful, quiet, tree, owl

The Moon

🌀 **Skill Focus:** Reading Compound Words

Help students recognize compound words by encouraging them to use sticky notes during independent reading. When they encounter a compound word, they should write it down. At the end of a reading session, have each child bring his or her sticky note to the chalkboard. Write each of the words on the board for a discussion. This is a good activity for beginning readers because it forces them to monitor their own reading, gets them up and moving at the end of the reading session, and allows everyone to be an active part of the lesson.

New Words: daylight, really, light, upon, sky, circle, letter, ball, nothing, flag, when, nighttime

> *Related Lesson*
> See additional lesson on Reading Compound Words in "Sam cannot play" on page 24.

Who Is Out at Night?

🌀 **Skill Focus:** Using Context Clues

Teachers often talk about context clues, but we rarely give students practice in using them. This lesson offers that chance. The directions instruct the parent to read the story first, with the child providing words that make sense. Even if the words the child provides are not on the list, chances are great that the words will make sense in the context. Even young readers can do this correctly because of their knowledge of the syntax of the English language.

The *syntax* of a language is the way words are put together to make phrases and sentences. For example, in some languages the noun precedes the adjective ("the rose red"), but in English the noun follows the adjective ("the red rose"). Students learning English as a second language often transpose these words because

> *Related Lesson*
> See additional lesson on Using Context Clues in "Sam and a toy" on page 22.

they have not yet learned English syntax, but native English-speaking children will almost never do so. Rules like this are learned very early in language development.

New Words: should, alone, get, person, take, new, hunt, eyes, catch, class, feathers, bite, kinds, hand, listen, sound

The Picnic

Skill Focus: Identifying Words With the Letter *a*

In this week's assignment, students will be finding words that have the letter *a*, and then grouping them by category: words with /ā/; words with /ă/; or words in which the letter *a* is used to spell a different sound. You may find that students disagree about the placement of certain words in the answer columns. Regional dialects and accents can cause a lot of discussion on this topic. For the most part, the words in the "not long or short" column are those that are neither distinguishable as a clear and definite /ā/ as in *ape*, or /ă/ as in *apple*, or words that have 'silent' letters, as in *peach*. Be prepared to adjust what you consider as "right" depending on your location or your students' accents.

New Words: picnic, asked, mother, potato, chips, heard, nest, hurt, babies, inside

Potatoes

Skill Focus: Identifying Antonyms

Help students further develop their understanding of antonyms by playing "Simon Says"—with a twist. This time the game is "Simon Says *Opposites*." If you say, "Simon Says, 'Stand up,'" students must do the opposite and sit down. Children usually have great fun with this game because they have to think before they move. Enjoy the game and don't take it too seriously!

New Words: man, mad, yelled, cook, fat, soft, thin, crunchy, loved, pleased, few, sold, everyone, more, started, company, lots

Related Lessons

See additional lessons on Identifying Antonyms in "Sam is up" on page 36, and "The Rabbit and the Turtle" on page 84.

Jeans

Skill Focus: Stating the Main Idea

Sometimes readers can glean the main idea of a passage, but still have difficulty putting it into a sentence that succinctly states it. This activity provides practice in doing just that. You may want to repeat this process in other main idea lessons, because it is a particularly effective technique. When put together in a sentence, the answers to your carefully crafted questions help students create a main idea statement. Even though you will not be there to guide students and craft the questions during independent reading, the skills they gain in this activity can help them state the main idea more effectively when they are working on their own.

New Words: wear, jeans, first, find, gold, strong, pants, tear, special, cloth, from, brown, blue, denim, found, better, today

Parents, For Your Information: 126 words, 6 new words—
their, sun, shine, still, made, rainbow

LISTEN to your
child read this
story aloud.

Sad Day, Happy Day

Maria and Michael were in the house *looking* out. It had *rained* and *rained* all day. Maria and Michael did not <u>play</u>. They did not <u>laugh</u>. They did not <u>call</u> their friends. They just *looked* as it started to <u>rain</u>. They *looked* and *looked*. The sun did not <u>shine</u>. It *rained* and *rained*. It was a sad day.

Then out came the sun! It was still *raining*, but the sun was *shining*. It *shined* on the rain and made a rainbow. Maria and Michael went out to <u>play</u> in the rain. They *called* to their friends, "Come <u>look</u> at the rainbow." They were *playing* in the rain. They were *laughing* with their friends. They *played* and *laughed* all day. It was a happy day after all.

Week-by-Week Homework for Building Reading Comprehension and Fluency: Grade 1
SCHOLASTIC TEACHING RESOURCES

Dear Parents,

Notice that some of the verbs in this story are underlined. These words represent the basic form of the verbs (also called verb stems) that we start with before we add endings. All of the underlined verbs are repeated in the story with two different endings: -ed and -ing. You can help your child read these "new" words (shown in italics in the story) by covering the endings with your finger, asking your child to say the familiar word, and then moving your finger to reveal the ending. In most cases, your child will be able to guess the ending, because it is simply what makes sense in the sentence. Be sure to repeat the word all ways (play, played, playing) before going on to the next exercise.

Skill

Adding Endings to Verbs

We completed this assignment together.

_____
(Child's Signature)

_____
(Parent's Signature)

The Questions

Look at this list of action words (verbs). Each one of them is a base word. Sometimes we put endings on base words. There are lots of them in this story. Look at the base words here and look back at the story. Then write the words with their endings.

Base Words	With -ed ending	With -ing ending
look	_____	_____
rain	_____	_____
play	_____	_____
laugh	_____	_____
call	_____	_____
shine	_____	_____

Parents, For Your Information: 135 words, 23 new words—dirt, may, earthworm, funny, have, arms, legs, bones, ears, nose, teeth, leaves, tunnel, move, rock, air, make, plants, grow, need, our, where, walk

After the Rain

One day after the rain, go outside. Go outside and look in the dirt. You may see an earthworm. Earthworms come out of the dirt after the rain. The earthworm is funny. It does not have arms or legs or bones. It cannot make noise. It does not have ears or a nose or teeth.

The earthworm is a good friend. It eats dirt and leaves. It digs a tunnel in the dirt. An earthworm is little, but it can move dirt and it can move a big rock. It moves rocks and dirt to make tunnels. Rain and air go in the tunnels. Rain and air make plants grow. We need the earthworm to help our food grow.

Look where you walk after the rain. Do not walk on a good friend, the earthworm.

Week-by-Week Homework for Building Reading Comprehension and Fluency: Grade 1
SCHOLASTIC TEACHING RESOURCES

Dear Parents,

This piece may well be one of the first purely nonfiction articles that your child has read. It contains only factual information about the earthworm. Most children love to learn about their natural world, but such nonfiction articles usually require a vocabulary that is too advanced for beginning readers. So it's important to include "real" nonfiction books when you are choosing material to read out loud to your child. Your child can understand hundreds of words that he or she cannot yet read.

Encourage (and help) your child to go back to the text to answer these questions. This kind of searching lays the groundwork for the advanced skills of skimming and scanning that older readers employ.

We completed this
assignment together.

_____
(Child's Signature)

_____
(Parent's Signature)

The Questions

Read the questions below. Use a crayon to underline the sentence in the story that answers each question. Then write the correct answers on the lines.

1. What does an earthworm eat? _____

2. What does the earthworm dig in the dirt? _____

3. When does the earthworm come out of the dirt? _____

4. How does the earthworm help us? _____

_____

Parents, For Your Information: 131 words, 15 new words—
know, name, say, colors, always, must, same, time, your,
sunlight, red, top, orange, guess, use

LISTEN to your
child read this
story aloud.

Roy G. Biv

Do you know Roy G. Biv? Roy is not real, but his name will help you say the colors of the rainbow.

We do not always see a rainbow with rain. To see a rainbow we must have sun and rain at the same time. To see the rainbow, you must have the sun shining on your back. The sun shines on the rain and lets us see the colors in sunlight.

Red is always at the top of the rainbow. That is the R in Roy. Then comes orange. That is the O in Roy. Can you guess what color is next?

The next time you see the sun and the rain at the same time, look for a rainbow. Use Roy G. Biv to help you name the colors.

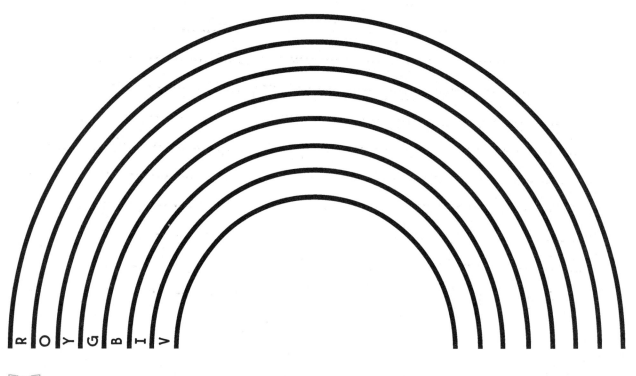

Week-by-Week Homework for Building Reading Comprehension and Fluency: Grade 1
SCHOLASTIC TEACHING RESOURCES

Dear Parents,

In an acronym, the first letter(s) of each word in a phrase or string of words is combined to make a new word. One common acronym is radar (radio detecting and ranging).

This homework assignment helps your child learn how an acronym works. Make sure your child realizes that Roy G. Biv is not a real person, but a name we've made up to reflect the order of the colors in a rainbow.

You can make this easier for your child by having him or her lay out crayons in this order: red, orange, yellow, green, blue, indigo (which is a really bright blue) and violet (which your child will call purple, so you'll need to explain). Then let your child look at the first letter of the color names that are printed on each crayon to discover the name Roy G. Biv.

We completed this assignment together.

_____

(Child's Signature)

_____

(Parent's Signature)

The Questions

Look at the name Roy G. Biv. Beside each letter of the name, print the color that this letter stands for. Then use the letters in the name Roy G. Biv to help you color the rainbow on page 74 correctly.

R _____

O _____

Y _____

G _____

B _____

I _____

V _____

Parents, For Your Information: 136 words, 7 new words—
night, stars, moon, beautiful, quiet, tree, owl

A Night Walk

One night Father said,   Let's go for a walk. We can see the stars and the moon. The night is beautiful.

Maria and Michael walked with Father. They walked and walked. Then they came to a field. It was still and quiet.

Father said,   Look at the stars and the moon. The moon looks big and the stars look little.

Michael said,   The moon is beautiful. It can shine in the night.

Then there was a noise. Maria and Michael did not know what it was. They looked up in the tree. It was a beautiful owl. The owl made a noise.   Whooo, Whooo, said the owl.

I like the noise of the owl,   said Maria.

Now we will go back to the house, said Father.

It was a beautiful night for a walk,   said Maria.

Week-by-Week Homework for Building Reading Comprehension and Fluency: Grade 1
SCHOLASTIC TEACHING RESOURCES

Dear Parents,

Even capable readers sometimes have difficulty with the punctuation that indicates conversation. Help your child with this activity by taking turns reading the dialogue. The first time through, read the father's part yourself, and have your child read the words spoken by the children. The second time, you may want to switch roles. Make the owl noises together, to make the experience more fun!

Your reading will be far more effective if you add exaggerated voice inflections. Make Father's voice very deep and the children's voices very high, squeaky, bossy, or slow. The more you do to make reading fun for your child, the more he or she will want to read. The more children read, the easier it becomes for them. There is no substitute for experience when it comes to building reading fluency.

We completed this assignment together.

_____
(Child's Signature)

_____
(Parent's Signature)

The Questions

❋ • • • • • • • • • • • • • • • ❋

In this activity we will use colors that universally mean "stop and go," red and green. Each time someone in the story starts talking, add green quotation marks. When that person stops talking, add red quotation marks. Repeat this each time a new person or animal starts and stops talking throughout the story.

LISTEN to your child read this story aloud.

The Moon

Look up into the sky. Can you see the moon? You can see the moon in the daylight or at night. The moon does not really shine. The sun shines on the moon and makes it look light. Sometimes the moon shines the sunlight down upon us. It is beautiful in the moonlight.

The moon moves around in the sky. Sometimes the moon looks like a circle and sometimes it looks like the letter C.

What is on the moon? The moon is a ball of rocks and dirt. There is no air or rain or food on the moon. There is no noise. Nothing can grow on the moon. No one can live on the moon, but people did go there. They went to see the rocks and dirt. Now there is a flag from the U.S.A. on the moon, but you cannot see it when you look up in the nighttime sky.

Dear Parents,

The first homework assignment on compound words included only two examples. Look how far your beginning reader has come since then. Notice the volume and complexity of the reading material your child is now working with. Most parents (and teachers) are both proud and amazed at the rate at which young children typically learn to read.

Today's lesson actually contains two kinds of compound words—those that join two separate nouns (moon and light become moonlight) and those that combine a word pair for ease of spelling and pronunciation (no thing becomes nothing and in to becomes into). Be sure to point out compound words in all your child's reading as he or she continues to advance through more complicated stories and materials.

Skill

Reading Compound Words

We completed this assignment together.

_____
(Child's Signature)

_____
(Parent's Signature)

The Questions

There are nine different compound words in the story. Work together to underline them in the story and copy them here. One is done for you. (**Hint:** Some compound words are only four letters.)

__nothing__

Parents, For Your Information: 153 words, 16 new words—
should, alone, get, person, take, new, hunt, eyes, catch, claws,
feathers, bite, kinds, hand, listen, sound

READ this
story aloud
to your child.

Who Is Out at Night?

Use these words: teeth, claws, quiet, kinds,
feathers, eyes, food, day, mice, bite

Do you like to go out at night like
Michael and Maria? They went out
with their father. You should not go out
alone.

Get an older person to take you out
at night and you may see something
new. You may see an owl. Owls are up
at night and they sleep in the
_____. At night they hunt for
_____. They like to eat
_____. They can find mice with
their big _____.
They can catch mice with their _____. An owl has
_____. The feathers make it _____ when it
hunts for mice. They eat food in one big _____.
Owls have no _____.

There are 150 _____ of owls. Some are big.
Some are small. One owl is only as big as your father's
hand.

Go out at night. You may see a beautiful moon and
stars. You may see a beautiful owl. Just listen for the
sound "Whoooo, whooo."

Week-by-Week Homework for Building Reading Comprehension and Fluency: Grade 1
SCHOLASTIC TEACHING RESOURCES

Dear Parents,

Have you ever finished a sentence for someone? You are able to do this because you understand syntax—the way language works and is supposed to sound. There are certain words that logically fit into our sentences. You also use context clues to help you know what comes next.

This homework assignment is different from others you may have completed. You will be asking your child to furnish the words to complete sentences that you will read to him or her.

After all of the blanks have been filled in, ask your child to read the entire story out loud. He or she should be able to read the newest words because they make sense in the sentence and because the child has just written those words down.

We completed this assignment together.

_____

(Child's Signature)

_____

(Parent's Signature)

The Questions

This story is to be read out loud by an adult. Begin by looking at the list of words in the box on page 80. These words are mixed up, but they all belong in the story. Then read the story aloud. Each time you come to a blank, pause to see if your child can provide a word that makes sense. Then read it again, together, and help your child print the correct word in the space. Finally, see if your child can read the whole story alone with the new words in place. (Note: Your child may provide a word that is not in this list. As long as the word makes sense in the sentence, it's acceptable to use that word.)

Parents, For Your Information: 149 words, 10 new words—
picnic, asked, mother, potato, chips, heard, nest, hurt, babies, inside

LISTEN to your
child read this
story aloud.

The Picnic

Maria and
Michael wanted to
have a picnic. They
asked Mother to
help. They got
some grapes and
some potato chips.
They went out to
the big tree.

Michael and Maria sat down to eat. Then they
heard a noise. It was not a cat. It was not a dog.
The noise was in the tree. They looked up. Up in
the sunlight they could see a nest in a tree. They
could hear a loud noise. It was a mother bird. She
made noises at Maria and Michael. She was
afraid that Maria and Michael would hurt her
babies.

Michael and Maria got up. They went back
inside. They went in to have their picnic. They did
not want the mother bird to be afraid of them.
They had their picnic in the house. Maria and
Michael smiled. It was funny to have a picnic in
the house.

Dear Parents,

"Phonetics" is a linguistics term for the study of the sounds in our language. Phonics is a related term that refers to the association between spoken sounds and written symbols. Beginning readers learn to make links between sounds and the letters representing those sounds.

Phonics instruction works for many words in our language, and for those words children learn to decode the written symbols by using their knowledge of phonics. Many words, however, are irregular and do not follow the rules of phonics. These are referred to as sight words, meaning that the child simply has to memorize them.

This homework assignment is a phonics lesson about the letter a.. A "short a" sounds like the /a/ you hear in apple. A "long a" sounds like the /a/ in ape. All other words with a go in the third column.

We completed this
assignment together.

_____
(Child's Signature)

_____
(Parent's Signature)

The Questions

Use a red crayon to circle every word in the story that contains the letter *a*. There are three columns below. Working together, write each word that contains an *a* in the correct column. (**Hint:** You need to write each word only one time. There are just enough lines to write all the *a* words.)

Short *a*	Long *a*	Not long or short
have	grapes	Michael
		Maria

Parents, For Your Information: 153 words, 17 new words—
man, mad, yelled, cook, fat, soft, thin, crunchy, loved,
pleased, few, sold, everyone, more, started, company, lots

LISTEN to your
child read this
story aloud.

Potatoes

One day a man was eating. His potatoes were not good. He was mad. He yelled and yelled at the cook. He said, "The potatoes are too fat and too soft. The potatoes are bad."

The cook was sad. He made new potatoes for the man. The new potatoes were not fat. They were thin. They were not soft. They were crunchy.

The man loved the new potatoes. Now he was not mad. He was pleased. The cook was not sad. He was happy.

Then a man named Herman liked the crunchy, thin potatoes. He called them "potato chips." He made a few of the new potato chips and sold them. Soon everyone liked the potato chips. He sold more and more. He started a potato chip company. They still make potato chips. They make lots and lots of potato chips. Do you like your potatoes fat and soft, or thin and crunchy?

Week-by-Week Homework for Building Reading Comprehension and Fluency: Grade 1
SCHOLASTIC TEACHING RESOURCES

Dear Parents,

   This is the true story of the origin of potato chips. The man who did not like the soft potatoes was Cornelius Vanderbilt; the cook was a Native American named George Crum. In 1945 Herman Lay created the Frito-Lay® Company by merging his potato chip business with the man who made Fritos,® Elmer Doolin.

   This story provides great opportunities for your child to learn new words and to practice finding antonyms, words with opposite meanings. A couple of these answers are tricky, so please be prepared to scan the story for pairs of words that have opposite meanings.

We completed this assignment together.

_____
(Child's Signature)

_____
(Parent's Signature)

The Questions

This story has antonyms. Antonyms are words that mean the opposite thing, like *day* and *night* or *old* and *new*. Find the antonym for each word and write it on the space below.

hated _____   bad _____

old _____   sad _____

mad _____   happy _____

fat _____   few _____

soft _____   then _____

Parents, For Your Information: 136 words, 17 new words—
wear, jeans, first, find, gold, strong, pants, tear, special,
cloth, from, brown, blue, denim, found, better, today

LISTEN to your
child read this
story aloud.

Jeans

Do you like to wear jeans?
Do you know who made them
first?

Once a man went to
California to find gold. The
people there were looking for
gold. They were digging in dirt
and they needed strong pants
that would not tear. The man
got special cloth from France. It
was from a town called "de
Nimes." He made lots of pants
from the cloth. The people started calling the
cloth "de Nimes." The first pants were brown, but
the man made them blue.

The pants are called jeans and the blue cloth is
called denim. The man's name was Levi Strauss.
People say he did not find gold in California, but
he found something better. He made lots and lots
of jeans, and his company still makes them today.

Dear Parents,

Here's a tip to help you read and pronounce the name of the town in this story: In "de Nimes," the s is silent and the i is pronounced as /ē/, so the pronunciation is actually de neem. This sounds quite close to the way we pronounce the familiar cloth denim.

When students read a passage, they are often asked to determine the main idea of what they have just read. Help your child with this difficult skill by discussing and answering together the following questions before you attempt to do the activity below.

Who was the man in the story? _____

Where did he go? _____

What did he make for the people there? _____

What did they call the cloth? _____

We completed this
assignment together.

_____

(Child's Signature)

_____

(Parent's Signature)

The Questions

Use the answers to the questions above. Put them into the following blanks to create a sentence that is the main idea of this story.

_____ _____ went to _____,

and there he made _____ out of _____.

Bonus Lessons on Poetry

If you teach primary grades, you might not be aware that on standardized tests poetry is treated the same way as prose. Therefore all of the standards, or benchmarks, that apply to fiction and nonfiction stories can also be applied to poetry. Many teachers like to include poetry throughout the school year, using seasonal and holiday poems to enrich their instruction. Other teachers prefer to teach a poetry unit so that students can fully study this wonderful genre. You may want to intersperse the prose assignments with an occasional poetry lesson, or alternately, present this whole section toward the end of the year, after you are sure your students can read the prose passages. Whatever you choose, the following poems are intended to strengthen beginning readers' understanding and appreciation of poetry. Have fun with them!

(**Helpful Hint:** Try folding this section back before making copies.)

Parents, For Your Information: 106 words, 16 new words—owners, peeps, mistress, packing, case, floor, answer, phone, left, bedroom, ground, returns, 'neath, nervous, whimpered, sighed

LISTEN to your child read this poem aloud.

Monty

Monty the dog is not happy
  today,
He knows that his owners are
  going away.
He runs up the stairs and peeps
  'round the door,
His mistress is packing a case, on the floor.
She goes down the stairs to answer the phone,
Monty is left in the bedroom, alone.
He jumps in the case and starts digging around,
The clothes are flying out—and are now on the ground.
His mistress returns; Monty hides 'neath the bed.
"It's no good you hiding, I'll find you," she said.
Monty was nervous, he whimpered and sighed.
She looked at his face and laughed till she cried.

by Brenda Huckin

Dear Parents,

One look at the illustration will tell the whole story of this poem. Studying the illustrations is not "cheating"; instead, your child should use any illustrations or photographs to help set the stage for reading and making predictions about the story. Remember to discuss any illustrations accompanying a story or poem with your child before he or she reads.

When children have a visual idea of what they are about to read, certain images and concepts form in their minds. Then, when they encounter an unfamiliar word in the selection, they are more likely to make a logical guess than just a "stab in the dark."

We completed this
assignment together.

_____
(Child's Signature)

_____
(Parent's Signature)

The Questions

✳ • • • • • • • • • • • • • ✳

Read these questions together. Then write a one-word answer for each question. (**Hint:** You may need to read the poem again.)

1. What do you think a "case" is? _____

2. What do you think a "mistress" is? _____

3. What is the meaning of the word '*neath*? _____

4. What is the meaning of the word *whimpered*?_____

Bonus: The last line of the poem says the woman was crying.
Why was she crying?

_____

Parents, For Your Information: 54 words, 14 new words—
Queen, Hearts, tarts, summer's, Knave, stole, clean, King,
beat, full, sore, brought, vow'd, steal

The Queen of Hearts

The Queen of Hearts,
She made some tarts,
All on a summer's day.
The Knave of Hearts
He stole the tarts,
And took them clean away.

The King of Hearts,
Called for the tarts,
And beat the Knave full sore.
The Knave of Hearts
Brought back the tarts,
And vow'd he'd steal no more.

Mother Goose rhyme

Dear Parents,

Even in this modern age, children still need to be familiar with Mother Goose rhymes because there are so many references to them in literature. Here is a poem about the famous Queen of Hearts.

This is one of those poems that is easy to understand even though the words are unfamiliar to us. Present this poem to your beginning reader in several steps. First, read the poem aloud yourself, asking your child to try to figure out what happened in the poem. Now read it aloud in unison with your child. See if he or she can guess the meaning of the unfamiliar words. Finally, have your child read it alone, making sure afterward that any unclear words are now understood.

We completed this assignment together.

_____
(Child's Signature)

_____
(Parent's Signature)

The Questions

Go back to the poem to answer these questions. Be careful! Some of the questions are tricky!

1. What did the Queen of Hearts make?_____

What do you think that is? _____

2. What did the Knave of Hearts do? _____

What do you think a "Knave" is? _____

3. What did the King of Hearts do?_____

What do you think "full sore" means?_____

4. What did the Knave of Hearts promise? _____

In the poem, what word is used to mean promise? _____

Parents, For Your Information: 95 words, 19 new words—
deep, well, grasshopper, fell, by, kicking, thought, wetter, about, might,
known, drowned, dangled, hope, molasses, passes, handy, hopped, proper

The Grasshopper

Down
a
deep
well
a
grasshopper
fell.
By kicking about
He thought to get out.
   He might have known better
   For that got him wetter.

To kick round and round
Is the way to get drowned,
   And drowning is what
   I should tell you he got.
      But
      the
      well
      had
      a
      rope
      that
      dangled
      some
      hope.

And sure as molasses
On one of his passes
   He found the rope handy
   and up he went, *and he*
      it
      up
      and
      it
      up
      and
      it
      up
      and
      it
      up
      went
And hopped away proper
As any grasshopper.

by David McCord

Week-by-Week Homework for Building Reading Comprehension and Fluency: Grade 1
SCHOLASTIC TEACHING RESOURCES

Dear Parents,

Poems that tell stories are known as narrative poetry. This simple poem is about a grasshopper who gets stuck in a well but is able to climb a rope to escape. As your child reads this poem, see if he or she can figure out the meaning of words that may be unfamiliar. After the reading, ask what "dangled" might mean. If the concept is unclear, try dangling a string in front of your child to give him or her an image of the rope hanging into the well.

There is The main skill for this poem is retelling the events of the story in the correct order. Help your child go back to the poem to reread it in its entirety, and if necessary, to find information in the poem to order the events correctly.

There's something special about this poem that may confuse your child. After the italicized words and he in the last stanza, the reader must skip to the bottom of that column of words and read upward. This is an effective visual device that helps the reader better imagine the grasshopper's climb to freedom!

We completed this
assignment together.

_____
(Child's Signature)

_____
(Parent's Signature)

The Questions

After you read this story, think about what happened to the grasshopper. Now write four sentences to tell the four things that happened in the poem.

1. The grasshopper _____.

2. He _____.

3. Then _____.

4. At last he _____.

Answers

Answers to Questions on Page 15:

1. Sam 2. Accept any three of the following: play; run; sleep; eat; jump 3. a good cat

Answers to Questions on Page 17:

1. up a ladder 2. a cat 3. Answers will vary. Accept anything that is reasonable. Possible answers include: He jumped down because he was afraid of the cat he saw; because he was scared; because he was too high up; because he wanted to. Unacceptable answers might be that he heard a loud noise or that he was hungry. There is nothing in the text or illustrations to suggest that this might be the case.

Answers to Questions on Page 19:

here; He; He; here; sleep; sleep; here
Bonus: likes

Answers to Questions on Page 21:

Answers will vary according to interpretation. Possible answers:
Sam will go to the water. What will Sam do? Sam will see a cat. Sam is scared! Will Sam look down? Sam will run and run and run!

Answers to Questions on Page 23:

Answers will vary. Possible answers: "Oh no!" "Pop!" "Bang!" "Look out!" "No, Sam!" "Be careful!" "Bad, Sam!"

Answers to Questions on Page 25:

something; cannot. Other answers will vary.

Answers to Questions on Page 31:

The things that Sam and Scruffy do that are the same are run, eat, play, and sleep. Scruffy takes a bath and Sam does not.

Answers to Questions on Page 33:

Answers may vary somewhat. Possible answers: 1. run 2. play 3. go up 4. go down 5. go around and around 6. go in and out 7. sleep

Answers to Questions on Page 35:

Answers will vary. Sample summary sentence: Scruffy rode in the car and Sam was sad until he got back.

Answers to Questions on Page 37:

down; will not; sad; cannot play. Other answers will vary.

Answers to Questions on Page 39:

You should look for five main elements in the child's illustration: 1. Sam is in the doghouse. 2. Scruffy is in the doghouse. 3. They look happy. 4. They are looking out the door. 5. It is raining. You may choose to give extra credit if the child includes other details such as the house in which Sam lives, storm clouds, lightning, or wet fur.

Answers to Questions on Page 41:

1. Sam was sleeping. 2. Scruffy went for a ride in the wagon. 3. Sam did not want to ride in the wagon. 4. Sam was sleeping. 5. Answers will vary.

Answers to Questions on Page 43:

the, they, then, something, this, with, there
Bonus: Accept T.V. changer or remote control.

Answers to Questions on Page 45:

Answers will vary. Assess or give credit based on how well titles reflect the main idea of the story. The title should have something to do with food, a bone, cat food, or sharing, or, at least, Sam and Scruffy.

Answers to Questions on Page 47:

Sam to Scruffy: either "I like to sleep" or "I will sleep all day." Scruffy to Sam: "Come and play with me."

Answers to Questions on Page 53:

1. The lion helped the mouse by not eating him and by letting him go. 2. The mouse helped the lion by chewing through the ropes and setting him free. 3. He helped the lion because the lion had done him a favor. 4. Answers will vary. Possible answers include: Little animals can help big ones. When you are kind, others will be kind back to you. You never know when some little thing can save your life.

Week-by-Week Homework for Building Reading Comprehension and Fluency: Grade 1
SCHOLASTIC TEACHING RESOURCES

Answers to Questions on Page 55:

Regular Verbs: looked; stayed. Irregular Verbs: saw; went; ate; slept; came; sat; said

Answers to Questions on Page 57:

1. a girl 2. She kissed him. 3. They got married and lived happily ever after. Summary: One day a frog went to see a girl and she kissed him. They got married and lived happily ever after.

Answers to Questions on Page 59:

1. slow 2. fast 3. won, lost 4. sad, happy

Answers to Questions on Page 61:

1. The people come to scare the wolf off. 2. The people come to scare the wolf off. 3. The people do NOT come to scare the wolf off. 4. They think the boy is playing a trick again. 5. Answers will vary. Possible answer: Do not play tricks about serious things.

Answers to Questions on Page 63:

1. The fox wanted some grapes. 2. He changed his mind because he couldn't reach the grapes. 3. The fox said the grapes were sour because he could not have any. Answers will vary. Do not accept answers that could not be inferred directly from the text (for example, he tasted the grapes, he got some off the ground, or the bird shared some with him). The answers must be text-based, which means the child cannot add information that was not provided in the story.

Answers to Questions on Page 65:

2. bird 3. cat 4. dog 5. fox 6. lion 7. mouse 8. rabbit 9. turtle 10. wolf
Bonus: The mice wanted a bell on the cat so they could hear him coming.
None of the mice could put the bell on the cat because they were too afraid to go near him.

Answers to Questions on Page 71:

looked, looking; rained, raining; played, playing; laughed, laughing; called, calling; shined, shining

Answers to Questions on Page 73:

1. dirt and leaves; "It eats dirt and leaves" should be underlined. 2. a tunnel; "It digs a tunnel in the dirt" should be underlined. 3. after the rain; "Earthworms come out of the dirt after the rain" should be underlined. 4. Answers will vary. Possible answer: The earthworm helps us by making tunnels so that rain and air can help plants grow. Any or all of the following sentences may be underlined: "It moves rocks and dirt to make tunnels"; "Rain and air go in the tunnels"; "Rain and air make plants grow"; "We need the earthworm to help our food grow."

Answers to Questions on Page 75:

Children should write the correct color names beside each letter and color the rainbow correctly. The top color of the arc is red; the color in the bottom arc should be purple, or violet.

Answers to Questions on Page 77:

One night Father said, **Green** Let's go for a walk. We can see the stars and the moon. The night is beautiful. **Red**

Maria and Michael walked with Father. They walked and walked. Then they came to a field. It was still and quiet.

Father said, **Green** Look at the stars and the moon. The moon looks big and the stars look little. **Red**

Michael said, **Green** The moon is beautiful. It can shine in the night. **Red**
Then there was a noise. Maria and Michael did not know what it was. They looked up in the tree. It was a beautiful owl. The owl made a noise. **Green** Whooo, Whooo, **Red** said the Owl.

Green I like the noise of the owl, **Red** said Maria.

Green Now we will go back to the house, **Red** said Father.

Green It was a beautiful night for a walk, **Red** said Maria.

Answers to Questions on Page 79:

These words can appear in any order: daylight; sometimes; sunlight; upon; moonlight; nothing; cannot; nighttime; into

Answers to Questions on Page 81:

These words are in order as they should appear in the story: day; food; mice; eyes; claws; feathers; quiet; bite; teeth; kinds

Answers to Questions on Page 83:

Short *a*: have, asked, and, sat, cat, at, that back, had; Long *a*: a, grapes, potato, made, afraid, babies; Not long or short: Michael, Maria, want(ed), eat, heard, was, hear

Answers to Questions on Page 85:

loved; new; pleased; thin; crunchy; good; happy; lots; now

Answers to Questions on Page 87:

Levi Strauss; California; pants (also accept clothes or jeans); denim
Main idea: Levi Strauss went to California, and there he made pants (jeans) out of denim.

Poetry Bonus Lesson 1:

1. suitcase 2. an owner 3. under or beneath
4. cried
Bonus: She was crying because she was laughing so hard.

Poetry Bonus Lesson 2:

1. tarts; A tart is a small pie. 2. He stole the tarts. a little boy who plays tricks 3. He gave the Knave a spanking. "Full sore" means "all the way," "completely," or "until he was sore." 4. He promised not to steal again; "vow" or "vow'd"

Poetry Bonus Lesson 3:

Wording of answers may vary. Answers should approximate the following: 1. The grasshopper fell in the well. 2. He kicked around in the water and almost drowned. 3. Then he saw a rope and began to climb up it. 4. At last he got out of the well and hopped away.